LANTERNS IN THE
NIGHT MARKET

PRAISE FOR
Lanterns in the Night Market

"In the tradition of Elizabeth Bishop, Mary Morris poses questions of travel in her luminously attentive *Lanterns in the Night Market*. This peripatetic collection opens with a compelling invitation that also hints at a potential sadness, loss, or rootlessness. 'Take my hand' says the speaker. 'The past is gone.' What ensues is a gorgeous slide projector of place after place: 'everything *and* and *and*.' These are clear-eyed poems that gaze candidly at trouble and troubled places—taking in the complexities of history, politics, and environmental crisis. But these are also poems of immense gratitude—revealing a poetic joy within the gorgeously-rendered details and images. This is a lovely and powerful volume."

—LEE ANN RORIPAUGH, author of *tsunami vs. the fukushima 50*

"A poem in Mary Morris' gorgeous *Lanterns in the Night Market* begins, 'There is an atlas inside your body—a certain instinct toward discovery'; this collection is an invitation to explore the world, guided by a seasoned and astute traveler whose missives include dreams, memories, and visions, poems like carefully framed snapshots of Laos, Bangkok, Angor Wat, Beirut, Mexico, and elsewhere. Morris claims in the first poem, 'Invitation,' that 'the past is gone,' but in these poems it is not ignored or forgotten. Morris does not sidestep or avoid destruction, death, and decay in the past or the present, even while pointing over and over again to exquisite details. These poems display Morris' prowess with concentration and skillful compression. As radiant as the woman in 'Bioluminescence,' swimming on her 80th birthday, this book, too, glows with an eerie, captivating beauty."

—REBECCA ARONSON, author of *Anchor*

"Mary Morris casts light, reflecting the incandescence of the traveled world, the sensory invitations, the way we may feel another panel within us opening 'to drink tiny fits of dreams.' Here, to travel means to register yearning and to experience both beauty and suffering 'even if it hollows you, / stranger.' These far-reaching, luminous, exquisite poems chronicle plenitude, the blessings of attuned and generous observation, and what to make of our encounters: 'This is my torch: ink / to invent my way.'"

—LEE UPTON, author of *The Day Every Day Is* and *Tabitha, Get Up*

LANTERNS IN THE NIGHT MARKET

poems   Mary Morris

TRP: THE UNIVERSITY PRESS OF SHSU
HUNTSVILLE, TEXAS 77341

Library of Congress Cataloging-in-Publication Data

Names: Morris, Mary, 1953- author.
Title: Lanterns in the night market : poems / Mary Morris.
Other titles: Lanterns in the night market (Compilation)
Description: First edition. | Huntsville, Texas : TRP: The University Press
   of SHSU, [2025]
Identifiers: LCCN 2024028503 (print) | LCCN 2024028504 (ebook) | ISBN
   9781680034042 (trade paperback) | ISBN 9781680034059 (ebook)
Subjects: LCSH: Travelers--Poetry. | LCGFT: Poetry.
Classification: LCC PS3613.O7739 L36 2025 (print) | LCC PS3613.O7739
   (ebook) | DDC 811/.6--dc23/eng/20240624
LC record available at https://lccn.loc.gov/2024028503
LC ebook record available at https://lccn.loc.gov/2024028504

FIRST EDITION

Cover art: James McNeill Whistler, *Nocturn in Black and Gold—The Falling Rocket*, 1875.
Author photo by Kenneth E. Apt
Cover design by Cody Gates, Happenstance Type-O-Rama
Interior design by Maureen Forys, Happenstance Type-O-Rama

Printed and bound in the United States of America
First Edition Copyright: 2025

TRP: The University Press of SHSU
Huntsville, Texas 77341
texasreviewpress.org

For Ken

CONTENTS

III

Invitation

Would you like to come with me?
Take my hand. The past is gone.

Shall we buy tickets?
Pack like mystics?

Look! Here is a suitcase
with an ocean in it

called *voyage*.
Could we fly?

Will raindrops bite
the windows of the plane?

Time is a dialogue
of exodus and entrance.

Little fears and slow digestion.
Admit it, say you want to.

You have always sensed
a longing—visitations

with Archangels
above cloud cover, seraphim

in lightning storms, Gabriel
playing saxophone.

Concur. You crave to tango
in Argentina in two-four time,

your arms around a being
with wings. Trust me,

Provence swallows the atlas
with lavender in spring.

Would you like to come along?
Take my hand. The past is gone.

Instructions for a Traveler

Leave your limited perspective
at the border. Journey further

than the ordinary even if it hollows you,
stranger, in a troubled land.

Conjure faith in stars, your sea
legs. Trust in body language.

Eat from a tagine laced with saffron
at the crowded souk in Marrakesh.

Soak in mineral waters of a hammam
near a road to the Blue Mosque.

Cross tortuous basalt mountains
in order to discover the temple.

Make offerings to beggars and musicians.
Journey before dawn. Leave in the dark.

Learn to roll the tongue.
Find new sounds in the mouth.

For *ocean*, sign *Crossing*.
For *mountain*, say *Giant*.

Breathe in incense and freshly split
papaya, body heat, holy basil.

Discover an imaginary map.
Suffer the broken bed

and missed train. God speed.
Inshallah. Bring back visions.

Dancing in Lisbon

We enter a longing for bliss.
He holds my *Manueline* waist.

Two guitarists finger-pick their way
along the quick road of a song.

We dust the floor with our hems,
ignite the ground with tiny blue fires

so that the alcoholics in the bar
sober up for life, make

of themselves—as we had
on the torched road to compassion—

their very own pietàs of suffering.

The Young Roma from Andalusia

After three countries and seven museums
    we ended up at a tapas bar in Madrid.
The Spaniards grew weary of tourists,

    their selfies, drunken songs on *Plaza Mayor*.
We sipped red wine, swallowed sardines.
    Fingers of guitarists disappeared inside

a flutter of strings, wove song of ache
    and longing, caused us to crane our necks
forward, as if beckoned to remember

    episodes crucially important.
An older man recalled the third death
    of his mother. A young woman

relived the birth of her son.
    When the tempo changed, the dancers
stamped, heel and toe into a rain-like staccato,

    pulled birds from the night air
with their curling hands. *Olé*,
    but it was the young Roma from Andalusia

in an erotic burlesque, his back to us
    as he flexed each glute to the music,
thrashed his head, reached to the sky, snapped

his fingers slowly, torqued his body
into that seductive profile that said, *Touch me*,
    here, while his shoes fluttered

with so much friction they sparked,
    then flamed. All slid from the cantina, rushed
back to their rooms, married the next day.

    Castilian roses unfastened their grips
of gold petals. Orange trees perfumed the boulevard.

Lorca's Lover

In forest
the lover's neck
is a young branch.
The breast, an orchard
he kneels into.
His mouth, a grotto—
temple of joy. Place
where bodies scissor
in grass, rise at the forested
torpor of animals,
at the green heart
of campesinos
praying at the gate for rain
in Granada, a city embedded
with *duende*, canciones,
crucifixions set with tourmaline
while fingers of savants
pluck guitars built from groves
of cypress in early June.
Yes, to the yearnings
of flamenco dancers.
Yes, to living in caves
painted with bison.

Lascaux

Sleep little cave girl

That you may have blown
    red pigment over those hands
        leaving prints of your existence

Left tools   torches   paintings
    of bison   talismans
        ephemera for your children

That part of you should always lie
    in the ground inside
        the womb of this cave

where once you rubbed two sticks
    blowing spark
        into fire

Freud in Paris

Gargoyles unfold their accordion wings,
    lift from ledges of Notre Dame,
hover above copper domes.

A blue house smolders red.
    The birthmark is a shadow
from the mother, a stamp

attached to its letter.
    Under the breast of a moon,
hypnosis takes your mind in its hands.

You doze, wearing your father's
    wedding dress of snow.
If you slumber at the edge of a cliff

you are forced to fly. Freud
    sleeps in the Latin Quarter,
dreams of death. At night, bobbing

on the Seine, a corpse
    bumps up against a houseboat,
knocking at the door of tenants.

Where the Bones of Lorca Sleep

Far from bullfighters.
Close to freedom fighters.

In land green as the ink
he wrote with.

Malachite, Pyrenees, new buds
in forest, foliage, rare orchids.
Lead bullets embedded in bone.

Through scrolls of hills redolent
with mint, dotted with Andalusian horses.

Beneath pulpit of an olive tree
occupied by goldfinch
singing in the firmament—
as each leaf, a calligraphy
in air, emerald in its radiant
anxiety, arouses.

Sprung from ballads of *gitanos*
within caravans, nomadic, migrating
over the belly of earth. In a biology
of taboo, desire unavoidably
meeting the forbidden, descended
from vermillion, marrow, blood
weddings, man to man to moon.

In the sea, a spectrum
of turquoise, bioluminescence.

In gardens of fireflies,
the earth fertile with Moors
where a shovel lies under ivy
and mud, digging its way
out of the grave.

Let him. *Let him breathe.*

I Read the Newspaper

to remember how wicked the world is
and novels to briefly escape it

which is why   in the green-leafed
morning   I read the *Times*

in the blue evening   Marquez
and before sleep   throughout

the day   crawl   from burnt tunnels
into the luminescent   country of poems.

The Art of Closeness

Near Istanbul, dolphins
were seen again
crossing the Bosphorus

while feral boar wandered
through pandemic Barcelona
snorting at the feet of Gaudí's Cathedral.

Rushing in from glade, herds of goats
grazed through city parks in Wales.

Sing them back—the shy shore birds
on Venice's Treporti Peninsula,
the monarch, junco, and honeybee.

Yes, praise the bees, buzzing
with a force not heard since first
we heard of their vanishing.

Cellist Playing Bach in Angkor Wat

Because its body is large as a human,
the musician embraces it
like a lover, caressing the neck
as his other arm bows across
low, long deep notes.
We follow. Head first,
then feet. Held there, collecting
loss, limbs caught inside
the sequence as if looking out
so utterly far, it takes you
outside of yourself.
Rice fields.
Killing Fields.
Khmer Rouge.
A flurry of saffron-robed monks.
Landmines.
Mass cremations.
Your parents, their deaths.
The long last note, Jon
and you return from the past
into the present.
Forgiveness—the ultimate
way of Buddhism, you say.
And we continue walking,
walking toward another
temple. Then another.

Bangkok

Across from the flower market of marigolds—
shades of tangerine, honey, apricot.
Fragrant jasmine and lilies.

Past the burning of *joss* paper, an enormous banyan
with a wide gold ribbon
wrapped around its trunk.

A saffron-robed monk, aware of my eyes, staring
at this tall forest of one, nods, and says,
Spirits reside inside old trees.

A pregnant woman places flowers at its roots.
I scatter purple orchids there.

A gospel of boys
chant prayers.

Laos

We stay at the prison turned hotel,
    ride our bikes on the banks of the Mekong,

offer rice and mango to orange-robed monks
    who fill their begging bowls.

Scaffolding a mountain—thirty-five temples
    hived with human chanting.

In the Cave of a Thousand Buddhas—shrines.
    Candles flicker for the end of suffering.

Laos, once apocalyptic, most bombed country
    in war-plotted history.

Writers in Exile

When banished, she will not feel separate
but feed the hungry pages

of an empty book, traveling
as a caravan across paper.

In the journal, he may become destitute—
frail, roused, reduced.

The twenty-seven bones of a hand in an X-ray—
like small candles lit in the dark.

What the skeletal will carry,
create, destroy, hold.

Nerve endings of fingers fly
from the map of the shy brain

as they cover the continent
of a distant hemisphere, rush

the didactic hum of escape
routes, electrifying circuits.

Imagine them becoming impulse
or the way you move

your hand as a wand
through another's hair.

Raft

There is an atlas inside your body—

a certain instinct toward discovery
that desires nothing in return.

How did we arrive at this refuge, listening
to questions in another language?

How did they descend to this shelter
with a different view of the same water—

this room opening its doors
into the sapphired space before them—

temples below, not nearly as ancient
as this smoking volcano?

One might drink tiny fits of dreams
from cups painted cobalt blue

and citron, sip coffee brewed from beans
grown in their own country

while others hang on
to a splintered raft drowning.

Dinner with the Dictator

A bisque of nightingale tongue—
its last song still singing in cream.

Pâté of Pacific blue whale
garnished with confit of shark fin.

Tartare of white rhino flown in
yesterday morning from Kenya.

Mature eggs of ruby-throated
hummingbird, collected through
diminutive nests last evening.

Reindeer heart over a bed
of ancient sequoia root, unearthed
from vanishing forests of California.

Nearly extinct variety of honey bee
in a cake of shaved heron beak
layered with livers of snow geese.

Cordial from the blood of a saint.

London

The body of a queen
is carried through Westminster Abbey.

Below the floor lie tombs
of Newton, Darwin, and Hawking.

One can still sense Churchill
and the bombings

as a waitress from Ukraine
serves sushi in the evening.

Milliners of Sierra Leone sell stacks
of pork pie, fedoras, and driving caps.

World commerce conducts its business
from 17th-century wooden edifices

and high rise, modern glass buildings
while an enormous ferris wheel

called the London Eye spins above
the River Thames.

History shifts in its waters. Sonnets
of Shakespeare repeat in theaters.

LaGuardia

There are no angels in airports
though demons linger
among bars, drinking time
down to melted ice, swirled
with bourbon-soaked cherries
stabbed by tiny red swords,
ginned olives, or tequila sodden
limes, while passengers stand
in long, anxious lines, until hearing
ALL FLIGHTS ARE CANCELED
before returning home.
Devils delightfully rearrange
arrivals, belie departures.
They oppose the mortal airborne,
call into question humans
attached to flying machines—
that whole idea of soaring
above cumulus, lightning.
That much closer to seraphim.

Angel at the Station

From the window
of a train car
pulling away

I bear witness
to a lone figure
inside a crowd

where the hungry
and oppressed
gather round

She stands
heavily winged
iridescent

wearing a halo
of neon green

keeps one eye open
the other closed
before disappearing

Travelogue

Up to my ankles
in a swale of oysters,

I clutch black pearls,
trace the Mediterranean's

blueness in Turkey
and Van Gogh's farmers

carrying on their backs
the golden wheat of Arles.

I keep notebooks
in the south of France,

on the Pacific Rim,
east of the clouded moon—

poems, maps, scribbled graphs,
sketches of the past.

This is my torch: ink
to invent my way.

Ode to a Suitcase

Dear valise, holy roller, packed
carryall, my little Alhambra—
cracked leather stitched like a wound.
Origami of shirts folded to fish and bird.

Towed on back, hoist and heave, hauled
nomadic in lines long with weariness,
lugged from mountain town to airport,
crossing an ocean toward a distant continent.

I unfasten your teeth, open your jaw
at Customs under fluorescent and starlit
airports in Oaxaca and Serengeti
where we have both been searched

for forbidden apples and illicit drugs, X-rayed,
combed by swift hands, spidering layers,
then sniffed by wolf-sized German shepherds.
Haunted. Haggard. Sea salt gathered.

Scent of Andaman. Shirt fragrant
with smoke of banyan, curry, lavender,
cinnamon. Scarf and hat possessed
by musk, vanilla, coffee, cardamom.

Sifted with red dirt, black sand,
Jamil's address. A seashell, empty.
Blue pashmina, stamped postcard
flamingo, lone silver drachma

at your depths. A peso, a euro
forgotten in a pocket, you have been
lost, found, unpacked, packed again,
snapped shut.

Shepherdesses of the Atlas Mountains

Wind removes scarves
from their heads as girls scale quartz and granite,
lead flocks of sheep, sleep under constellations
with their ewes and ram whose wool will be sheared,
spun, dyed indigo and saffron.

Children roll pastry, dotted with pistachio and honey,
collect mint for tea. Husbands slow-cook tagine
of preserved lemon, apricot, dates, and cumin.

When men return to the mountain to slaughter lambs,
women tighten head coverings
under their necks again.

Postcard, Marrakesh, 4 a.m.

Dark street.
Scent of saffron.

Nighthawk flies above
strum of an oud.

Twelfth century mosque.
An empty souk.

I Listen to Bees

like the call to prayer

under eaves—
of a paper-thin mosque

where they return
five times a day

Oceanic

If seventy-one percent of the earth's surface
is water—if what we see is only a fraction

If the gods give   but also take away
like the purple sock in the waves

caught in my hand   or the plastic bag
that bumps up against my mask—

periphery endless   excess dangerous
If beauty reeks ugly   If the storm

cleans one beach   pollutes another
If the polyurethane bottle

from the Sea of Java turns up
in the Sea of Bali   what then

of *us*   What of the *where?*
What especially   of the *why?*

This puffer   speckled   and boxfish
square like its name   A snowflake eel

tucked inside its coral den   darting
its tiny head   in my mind hereafter

The ebony and white manta ray   large
as a boat   soars above this human body

in slow motion—fanning its wings
graceful as an angel for a mariner

Don't Lose Sleep

over the possibility of heart attacks or cancer.
At any moment we could all be destroyed

by an asteroid or any other type of disaster—
a new virus, an old disease, choking on an apple.

Love, swim the backstroke out to sea
in the district of joy, where boats sail

and fishermen gaze, or over a coral reef
that hasn't died yet.

His last breath was this: an ocean we rowed through
in the Pacific where dolphins followed.

If I loved you any more, I would die of an overdose.
It chars—this departure, explosion, confetti of lost objects.

A field guide to grief, the honeycombed skull.
We are endangered. And yet—

the emerald grass skitters across the umber earth.
A skulk of kit fox inhabits the arroyo

where the coyotes once were. Risk
everything. Effect of contradiction.

The blue-gold lake. Loss is the journey
where we arrive still drenched.

Let's clean this tiny stretch of beach overnight.
Come susurrant unarmed with wet eyes bright.

Love in the Time of Insurgency

In memory of civilians

When they bomb the hospitals,
homes, mosques, limbs severed by shrapnel

fly through the air—ghost limbs, fingers
point here, over there, insinuate

everywhere, nowhere. Darling,
only a lone slab of preservation left.

In my dreams, I unmoor a boat
from banks of the Tigris, where fish

will feed us, hum in our bellies.
Where I serve carp with scattered stars of salt

on a moon-round plate. Pick up
your slack, love, before the cart of the dying

takes you slow as a donkey
through the opposition road. Baghdad,

once called *Given Garden*, now a desert
stolen. Babylon—all the walls

come tumbling, come tumbling down.

Beirut

A man reads a newspaper on the sixth floor.
He looks up and out at the open-air —
once a wall, now an overhang, cliff of brick
bombed last month. He has become
accustomed to this. The man sips
a glass of tea, warm and fragrant with mint
inside the tall building, exposed.
He has always been exposed. His people,
the story, ancient. Beyond the dead.
One must believe in wind if not in dirt.

Lanterns in the Night Market

A baker opens doors to his clay oven,
pulls loaves of bread scented with onion.

Flesh of fresh-cut watermelons gleam
like organs. Torches lit above rows

of pomegranates. Pyramids
of saffron glint, gild dark corners.

A man drums, a woman sings.
Children dance until they sleep.

Nighthawks dip, suturing the sky
with dreams.

Take Five

—*after the Dave Brubeck Quartet*

In Amman, Jordan, three women smoke
lemon scented *shisha* on a balcony.

Five musicians appear from the jazz festival.
A dialogue begins with a piano in five-four time.

Enter whisk and marching beat from that bass drum,
piano rhythm, intoxicating saxophone, a woman—

her voice scatting—all together, generating
music so intimate, it's like being in love.

Dave Brubeck has returned from the dead.
Hundreds of people leave the street, gather
on these wide steps at the University of Petra.

Taxi drivers from Palestine abandon their cars
to join us. Music unites all into one language.

Take five, take five on your busy day.
To find someone. To notice.

To believe in the world
as *us*.

The Red Desert

What we find here: a map to the stars.
Giant monoliths carved by wind.

A vast valley of scattered Bedouin
who invite us in.

We camp in the Valley of the Moon
at Wadi Rum, its rippled sand dunes

of iron-rich red oxides. Stand
at the highest edge on a plateau

of the Arabian Desert, watch
a string of yellow dromedaries
sway across the horizon.

In the book of Exodus, three
thousand years before, forty
miles away, Moses parted the sea.

In this dazzling landscape—cliffs
etched with ancient petroglyphs

of lion, monkey, elephant, pre-
Sumerian poems—a thousand
inscriptions of mystery—

we sleep.

Bioluminescence

At night, off the coast of Turkey
nestled between ruins of Olympus

and the Taurus Mountains—the sea
lights up with neon plankton

so that the woman who dives, splashing
off the bow of our boat, swims,

divides, cresting her own
galaxies and constellations—

a Milky Way encircling her body
aglow, mesmerizing all on deck.

It is her eightieth birthday.
Yes, she is radiant.

Istanbul

Hustling through a bustling market
fragrant with coffee, saffron,
and frankincense, we encounter
four women buying pomegranates,
reminding us of Persephone in a city
so feminine within its rounded *hammams*—
their pink, sixth-century domes.

Outside the Blue Mosque, men wash
their feet under a spigot. Minarets
announce a third call to prayer.
All find their places to pray—in
the market, street, park, hammam.

By evening near the Hippodrome,
between sips of Turkish coffee,
we feed each other paper thin pastries
laced with green pistachio and honey.

We play backgammon with rug vendors
under sea-glass lanterns, move checkers
on tapestries thick with wool dyed
crimson, above a thin scent of lanolin.

A sultan once ruled this municipality
once known as Constantinople,
Ottoman's Empire. In his Topkapi
Palace, he kept hundreds of concubines

and eunuchs to protect them.
So anxious about assassination, he slept
each night in a different location.

Now, a museum exists, where power
has been reduced to a few humble relics
of Muhammad—a fingernail, his beard
and the blessed bowl he drank from.

Dreaming Khashoggi

If the soup hisses back
be suspicious.

If you believe their aim
is to smuggle

your body parts
from the building,

command
your angels.

Dream of your fiancée
holding you in future

perfect,
in the constant

birth and burning
of stars.

Dreaming down the Bosphorus

between shores
of the Aegean

and Black Sea, we sail
over an ocean of amber
beneath this lip of water.

On land, we explore ruins,
ghosting through ancient
doors of forgotten tombs.

Africa

This is moonlight, baroque,
the legend of his shoulders

poised in a landscape
of holy existence, our clothes

flung across the tent, dusty
from the Serengeti, sand

slowly emptying into grooves
between planks of the wooden floor.

Outside, rustle of hippos.
Near the door, a lion roars.

Full Moon Over Serengeti

Serengeti is a Masai word
meaning *endless plain*.

Within jacaranda, its sweet scent—
numerous pairs of eyes.

The Serengeti is *always* alive.
Sound of wood owls carry through acacias.

A leopard draped on branches
chews its kill.

Great thirsty herds of wildebeest
gaze at the Mara River

in their prolonged deliberation
of crossing the treacherous.

The full moon shines its radiance
on all nocturnal.

A ghostly flower
blooms in the dark.

Albino Afrikana

They thought she was a ghost, a man.
She was more than.

She was in the middle of the Serengeti
stirring witch-wood soup.

There was a nest on top of her head
with hatchlings.

She wore a bracelet of shell,
a Makonde mask, a necklace

of teeth from a lion she had eaten—
therefore, all kept their distance.

Camouflaged, she exposed
her pale hand, so the tribe did not

trust her. She wore a mask, as I said,
so all felt watched.

I first met her at a hotel
in Dar es Salaam.

She was working as a receptionist.
She was the outcast the manager took in.

Weary, wary, she did her job.
She showed us to our rooms

and slipped a smile, the kind
of giving in—one of an exile.

Kilimanjaro

If the ice melts

if the revelations arrive
too late

if the glaciers retreat

so do the gods

Zebra

Beasts, lords, angels, seraphs.
  Rustle in the grasses.
Pampas. Tundra.

Two hundred zebra
  cross the path
and no man can tame them.

They won't bite the bit,
  hold the saddle, will not
be restrained.

They defy domesticity
  unlike their cousin, the horse,
bridled by humans.

Not to be ridden or driven
  the striped beast refuses
even to appear as spirit

in a young girl's dreams.
  Two hundred zebra
gallop in freedom.

Serengeti, Kopje Rock Formations

From a landscape of enormous oblelisks
President Nyere moved an entire tribe

of Masai in Serengeti, in order
to save animals from extinction.

Nomad, lion-fierce, you stayed.
Nomad, you still have your red

shuka, a robe the color of blood
to frighten beasts with long teeth.

Your tall spear, sharp with protection.
Your will, like birds, resists relocation.

Arrivals and Departures

He journeys through India.
I reminisce.
His hands at my hip bones,
that ringtone of thirst.

If you come to Calcutta, he says,
bring your hand-me-down soul.
For the Untouchables, your
brightest magenta sari.

Shiva owns too many arms, I say.
When are you coming home?

He travels to Persia, learns Farsi.
His blood has turned to silk,
he says, a tapestry of empire
simmering with saffron.

Save me a pomegranate, I say.

* * *

In Egypt, a *khamaseen* sweeps through
the Sahara, while a driver steers
toward its stinging breath. Spiral
winds, a three-day inferno, singing

sandstorm in the key of G. Headlights
in daytime. Camels half-buried in dust.

By the time they reach Cairo, he's lost
his passport. Sadness is the thief

of patience. He discovers the embassy
of his native country, where an officer
stamps a green pyramid on his forehead,
ships him down the Nile.

For security purposes, I send a telegraph
in the hieroglyphics we invented, saying,

Next time, keep your original documents
in the pocket beneath the knife.

He laughs and visits a distant relative
of Nefertiti. Six months later, his clothes
hang in the closet like ghosts.
A collar trembles. A cuff quivers.

His shoes leave footprints across
the landscape of my dreams. My pillow
becomes a cloud above his corpus,
drifting down the lengthiest

tributary in a land of kings and queens,
preserved in natron, bitumen, honeycomb,
wax, and linen. I wake alone in darkness
to the burning of frankincense.

* * *

A dream is not a premonition
nor prophetic, but a tracking

from the brain stem to the cortex
a ripple through the amygdala—

the subconscious woven with fear.
A provision to keep alert. The knock
at the door in the interior of night.

Who's there?

Nocturne

I try to sleep, but the whispers

of my new lover are footnotes

attached to the bottom of my dreams.

The West Indies

A spider monkey screeches at dawn.

Palm trees tremble in tropics
above the sea.

We are rocked in waters
off Santa Lucia, an island

Derek Walcott wrote of, inside
one of the brightly painted houses on a hill.

Aqua   yellow   rose.

Poems scribed on barbaric history
of slave trading, plagued throughout

the Caribbean. Giving form
and order to cruelty.

Penned. Documented. Bleeding
poetry. Further up the beach—

an enormous skeleton of a whale—
its architecture resembling

magnificent arches inside a cathedral
where one could enter, be at peace.

The whale's organs and blood long gone
but the carcass, that construct—eternal

reminder of permanence. Walcott's
poems resonating timelessness.

Lava flowing from Volcano
Soufrière fuming in the distance.

Manatee

In the seventeenth century
the sailor saw

below the shadow
on the side of the bow

a mermaid
nursing her young child.

In Belize, green lagoons meander
where sea cows swim.

Sirenian herds languor.
Upriver, motorboats.

Danger.

The Dream, Frida Kahlo

Dear Death,

My nemesis, already we are sleeping together, dreaming above a field of lilies, flying above the house in clouds, our bones wired together by dynamite. I try to stay alive but the earth keeps burying me with vines. I paint green but am gessoed over. I lie down in peace, but the bed is charged with nightmares. You are in it. If one sleeps under a yellow blanket of pain, death is near. If the moon is white, it has teeth. Bite me. But let me sleep.

Amor,
Frida

Nest

Twice we built a nest in my cell-rich womb.
In one, the blood poured out in the boneyard.
We lived in Mexico. There were tiny candy skulls,
black hollows of eyes, a cemetery of wire cribs
and cries of mothers in black lace mantillas.

The second nest was Bach, passion, fugues
made for the salvation of dreams. When I moved
it went with me. There was this power
beyond my soul, *within*. What did I know
of bringing life or milk—something inside one.

I was a carrier, delivering. Carrier, caravan.
I was wet on the inside of my skin
with new skin. Vernix. Inside my body
was hair, another's ears. I listened to our fluids
and the beating of this extended heart. Love.

Mexico, the Dig

We light the candelabra, verdigris
from another century. Four beeswax
candles secured in its sockets
like chambers of the heart.

He is an excavator of bones, keeper
of secrets. From the cadmium basket
he selects clay artifacts—
a face, then a torso, discovered

in the irrigation ditch below.
When he joins them, they click
into perfect union. He becomes attached
to me, lights a fire, grills a sea bass

served with a poem inside its mouth.
Tonight, we dream in sonnets.

Vernacular

I am hungry for a language
from the mouth of a foreign country

where sound is a fountain I drink from
in small increments.

Where the word for flowers melt
into *flores* and green tastes *verde*.

We eat *pescado* while gazing out to sea.
Sí, and *la gente*, the people, are gentle.

Once, we caught fish all day.
You dove for *langosta*.

Once, this was home, a *palapa*
of thatched palms on a beach.

I learned the phrases slowly,
the people so patient with me.

Christina asking, *María, flaca,*
do you have any pescado para mi, hoy?

Mary, thin one, do you have any fish
for me today?

María, te gustaría una cerveza, un mango?
Mary, would you like a beer, a mango?

Tender Cristina, her small children
gathered around her skirt

as Jose's *pozole* simmered on the stove,
the entire sky ablaze.

Your Sister Visits Us in Mexico

They arrived on a Saturday, when villagers sold mango on sticks, a glowing fruit from Eden. Where yellow determined, received its name, and sweetness began. A color evoked by light, the sun. When Campesinos sold *chicharrones*, *pulpo*, *tacos al carbón* and old men at the market ate charred sweet potatoes, *huevos rancheros*, drank their coffee with cinnamon. Sunday was a feast day. A procession snaked through town. Some men carried a life-sized wooden god on a cross painted bloody, draped in a swath of white gauze. When the statue passed by, its eyes stared through you, wherever you stood. We drank fresh juice of tamarind, ate *pozole* on the porch of Don Juan and Elena María, while their children chased strutting roosters, clucking hens. Your sister and her husband insisted we drive fifty miles for a block of ice for their margaritas and martinis on the beach with no electricity. The butter melted. The salt caked into a little Utah. Let's drink to all the saints on an evening called *suffering*. Let's bring the dead back, paint their faces in our dreams called *remember*.

Day of the Dead

If you want to live in Mexico
you must understand
the hunger of the dead.
See them eat their life
in you, taste their bitter,
their butter, their honey, fish
caught early morning.
Cleaned and smoked.
Bones sucked.

You must shop at the mercado.
Fill your *bolsas* with mango,
avocado, beans, and tortillas.
Prepare their most desired
meals. Eat what you can.
Leave the rest for them.

Place this favored food on graves.
Return at dark, keep vigil. Light
many red votive candles.
Paint your face like a skull.
Be dead, dancing.

I Will Meet You at the Gateway

—the floating bridge,
past Alameda before
the diamondback bit the dog.

Down the *arroyo* where
our son became lost before dark.
That fire of the sun I wanted

to burn all night. Let us join
beyond the blood
in the body you died in.

Meet me. I will be there.
At the quarry of stone,
sunflowers and ashes.

Waiting.

Border Patrol

Are you documented?
Do you belong?

Where are your papers?
Do you exist?

Are you in possession
of authorizations, permits?

Who occupies you?
From where?

What possesses you?
How?

Once, I watched a border patrol
dismantle a family's Volkswagen

bus, seeking contraband.
Contra. Band.

You are under surveillance.
Hand over your nickels,

toothbrush, dirty clothes,
aura, soul.

Have an illicit apple
while you are being

detained. Herein lies
the garden of aliens.

Baggage

Tiny house on wheels
cobblestone quiverer—

holy burden, avatar
explorer—

shifting addresses
seeking shelter.

Displacement

When we lived in Mexico
brightly colored parrots flew

between hibiscus and palm,
and there were so many monarchs

they covered our arms, made of them
blazes of orange and black wings.

Hinges of small gold fires, opening
and closing—masses

migrating to New Mexico.
In Vermont this year, strangely

they rarely appeared. This winter
I spot the flicker of a lime-green

parrot in a cottonwood on Canyon Road.
It is thirty-two degrees and a stinging

wind blows. Soon, I see its owner
holding open a net as he calls

the tropical red-beaked bird to him
like a son.

Hotel Room

Lilac soap on a sink
wrapped as a present.

An empty closet
dark as a coffin.

The bed finished
carefully—sheets

crisp as an
envelope.

You dream. Still
you wake too early, turn

to catch the clock's
green illuminated numbers

counting the hours
before your departure.

NOTES

"Invitation": was inspired by James Galvin.

"Dancing in Lisbon": Manueline, also called Portuguese late Gothic, is a style of architecture that originated in Portugal in the 16th century.

"*Lascaux*": is a Paleolithic cave complex located in France.

"Postcard, Marrakesh": A *souk* is the name of a marketplace in North Africa or the Middle East.

"Arrivals and Depatrures": A *Khamaseen* is a lengthy and severe windstorm which occurs throughout the desert in the Middle East.

"Dreaming Down the Bosphorus": the Bosphorus is a natural strait in Istanbul connecting the Black Sea to the Sea of Marmara, forming one of the continental boundaries between Asia and Europe.

"Shepherdess of the Atlas Mountains": the Atlas Mountains are located across North Africa.

"Take Five": is a jazz song written by Paul Desmond, performed by the Dave Brubeck Quartet.

"Instructions for a Traveler": A *hammam* is a type of steam bath or place of public bathing in the Islamic world.

"Serengeti, Kopje Rock Formations": Kopje are ancient granite outcrops that rise above the grasslands of Serengeti.

"Dreaming Khashoggi": Jamal Khashoggi (1958–2018) was a Saudi dissident and journalist for *The Washington Post* who faced political persecution for his work. He was assassinated at the Saudi Consulate in Istanbul by agents of the Saudi government, allegedly at the behest of Saudi Crown Prince Mohammad bin Salman.

"Kilimanjaro": On October 19, 2021, the *New York Times* reported that the last three mountain glaciers in Africa are receding at such a rapid pace that they could disappear within two decades, a symbol of the broader devastation being wrought by climate change on the continent, according to a new U.N. report.

"*The Dream (of the Bed)*": is a painting by Frida Kahlo.

"Arrivals and Departures": lists methods and materials used in the mummification of bodies in ancient Egypt. Natron is a salt from dry lake beds. Bitumen is found in crude oil seepage.

ACKNOWLEDGMENTS

Arts & Letters: "The Young Roma from Andalusia"

Bending Genres: "Arrivals/ Departures"

Blue Mountain Review: "Ode to a Suitcase"

Book of Matches: "Freud in Paris"

Ekphrastic Review: "The Dream (of the Bed) Frida Kahlo"

Gargoyle: "Lorca's Lover"

Lily Poetry Review: "Postcard Marrakesh 4 a.m."

Lunch Ticket (Antioch University): "Vernacular"

Marrow Magazine: "Day of the Dead," "Nest," and "Shepherdesses of the Atlas Mountains"

New Mexico Discovery Award Anthology: "Africa," "Mexico, the Dig," and "I Read the Newspaper"

New York Quarterly: "Where Lorca Sleeps"

Nine Mile Magazine: "Invitation"

Nova Literary-Arts Magazine: "Take Five"

On the Seawall: "The West Indies," "London," and "Full Moon Over Beirut"

South Dakota Review: "Displacement"

St. Petersburg Review: "Love in the Time of Insurgency"

Stone Boat: "Bioluminescence"

Terrain.org: "Oceanic"

The American Journal of Poetry: "Dreaming Khashoggi"

The Comstock Review: "Instructions for a Traveler" and "Don't Lose Sleep"

The Museum of Trees Anthology: "Bangkok"

The Shore: "Lascaux" and "Raft"

Thrush: "Dancing in Lisbon"

Much gratitude to Kenneth Apt, J. Bruce Fuller, and Karisma Tobin.

Gracias to Richard Lehnert and Maggie Smith for their close reading and insight on this manuscript.

Many thanks to Tina Carlson, Deborah Casillas, Robyn Covelli-Hunt, Joy Jacobson, Donald Levering, Anne Haven McDonnell, Barbara Rockman, and Gary Worth Moody.

ABOUT THE AUTHOR

PHOTO BY KENNETH E. APT

Mary Morris is the author of three previous books of poetry: *Enter Water, Swimmer* (selected by X. J. Kennedy), *Dear October* (Arizona-New Mexico Book Award), and *Late Self-Portraits* (Wheelbarrow Book Prize). Her work has been published in *Boulevard*, *North American Review*, *Poetry*, *Poetry Daily*, *Prairie Schooner*, and *Rattle*. A recipient of the Rita Dove Award, *Western Humanities Review* Prize, and the National Federation Press Women's Book Prize, Mary has been invited to read her poems at the Library of Congress, which aired on NPR. Kwame Dawes selected her work for *American Life in Poetry* from the Poetry Foundation.